To Mummy and Daddy

Sense Poetry

Love from Chloe xx

Future Voices

Edited by Rob Harding

First published in Great Britain in 2016 by:
YoungWriters
Remus House
Coltsfoot Drive
Peterborough
PE2 9BF
Telephone: 01733 890066
Website: www.youngwriters.co.uk

Book Design by Spencer Hart

SB ISBN 978-1-78624-001-9

Printed and bound in the UK by BookPrintingUK
Website: www.bookprintinguk.com

Foreword

Dear Reader,

Welcome to this book packed full of sights and smells, sounds and tastes!

Young Writers' Sense Poetry competition was specifically designed for Key Stage 1 children as a fun introduction to poetry and as a way to think about their senses: what the little poets can see, taste, smell, touch and hear in the world around them. From this starting point, the poems could be as simple or as elaborate as the writer wanted, using imagination and descriptive language to conjure a complex image of the subject of their writing, rather than concentrating just on what it looks like.

Given the young age of the entrants, we have tried to include as many poems as possible. Here at Young Writers, we believe that seeing their work in print will inspire a love of reading and writing and give these young poets the confidence to develop their skills in the future. Poetry is a wonderful way to introduce young children to the idea of rhyme and rhythm and helps learning and development of communication, language and literacy skills.

These young poets have used their creative writing abilities, sentence structure skills, thoughtful vocabulary and, most importantly, their imaginations to make their poems come alive. I hope you enjoy reading them as much as we have.

Jenni Bannister

Editorial Manager

St Paul's and All Hallows CE Junior School, London

The Poems

Halloween Poem

H appy Halloween every vampire
A wesome and scary fun
L uminous costumes
L ittle spiders
O wls howling
W erewolves biting
E very ghost howls
E very vampire creeps through the street
N ever give up for treats.

Elqui Johnston (7)

Autumn

I see different coloured leaves
I hear crunching leaves on the ground
I smell the wet grass
I taste apples and vegetables
I feel the prickly conkers.

Oliwia Cios (5)
Birchwood CE Primary School, Warrington

What senses did you enjoy reading about on these pages? Colour the symbols.

Autumn

I see acorns hanging on the tree
I hear leaves crunching under my feet
I smell the vegetables growing
I taste a hot, hot chocolate
I feel the prickly conkers.

Erin Joyce Ingham-Harris (5)
Birchwood CE Primary School, Warrington

Autumn

I see the colourful leaves
I hear the leaves crunching
I smell the apples on the tree
I taste the fruit on the trees
I feel the leaves on my head.

Jaye Brown (5)
Birchwood CE Primary School, Warrington

What senses did you enjoy reading about on these pages? Colour the symbols.

Autumn

I see squirrels getting nuts
I hear my shoes crunching in the leaves
I smell the smoke by my hands
I taste the apples and the pears
I feel the hot wind.

Chelsea Davies (5)
Birchwood CE Primary School, Warrington

Autumn

I see conkers falling from the tree
I hear fireworks popping
I smell smoke in the house
I taste hot soup outside
I feel a prickly hedgehog.

Katie Bunt (5)
Birchwood CE Primary School, Warrington

What senses did you enjoy reading about on these pages? Colour the symbols.

Autumn

I see the leaves falling
I hear nice leaves crunching
I smell the smoke floating
I taste yummy soup
I feel soft leaves.

Alice Emily Bradley (5)
Birchwood CE Primary School, Warrington

Autumn

I see squirrels picking the acorns
I hear leaves falling on the ground
I smell the smoke from a chimney
I taste juicy apples
I feel warm in autumn.

Alex Jones (5)
Birchwood CE Primary School, Warrington

What senses did you enjoy reading about on these pages? Colour the symbols.

Autumn

I see acorns falling off trees
I hear birds tweeting
I smell the hot fire
I taste hot soup
I feel the leaves.

Kian Reynolds (5)
Birchwood CE Primary School, Warrington

What Is The Sun?

The sun smells like ice cream
The sun looks like a planet full of fire
The sun sounds like wood burning
The sun feels like getting burnt by a pan
The sun tastes like chicken chillies.

Carl Nathanael Kim (6)
Cameron House School, London

What senses did you enjoy reading about on these pages? Colour the symbols.

A Holiday

A holiday smells like sun cream
A holiday looks like sea creatures in the sea
A holiday sounds like squawking seagulls
A holiday feels like swimming in the pool
A holiday tastes like banana and strawberry smoothies.

Thomas Cagle
Cameron House School, London

Happiness

Happiness smells like pasta in a pan
Happiness looks like seal pups
Happiness sounds like pop music
Happiness feels like a kitten's soft fur
Happiness tastes like pizza covered in cheese.

Rex Kelly
Cameron House School, London

What senses did you enjoy reading about on these pages? Colour the symbols.

The Sun

The sun smells like a ball of smoke
The sun looks like a pancake coming out of the oven
The sun sounds like whooshing wind
The sun feels like a sparking fire
The sun tastes like ripe tomatoes.

Avantika Deshpande (6)
Cameron House School, London

What Is Chocolate?

Chocolate smells like melted caramel
Chocolate looks like a big plank of wood
Chocolate sounds like sparkling water blasting out of a bottle
Chocolate feels like a big frozen tissue
Chocolate tastes like sugar that is sweet.

Chiara Tondo
Cameron House School, London

What senses did you enjoy reading about on these pages? Colour the symbols.

What Are Flowers?

Flowers smell like a fresh summer's day,
Flowers look like someone coding a very fun video game,
Flowers sound like leaves swaying on a tree,
Flowers feel like cakes raining from the sky,
Flowers taste like sweet crunchy chocolate.

Joshua Kunchala
Cameron House School, London

What Is Happiness?

Happiness smells like apple juice.
Happiness looks like a heart.
Happiness sounds like peace and quiet.
Happiness feels nice and warm.
Happiness tastes like chocolate sweets.

Edward Pegg
Cameron House School, London

What senses did you enjoy reading about on these pages? Colour the symbols.

What Is A Holiday?

A holiday smells like children wearing sun cream.
A holiday looks like people swimming in the sea.
A holiday sounds like a cat miaowing on the beach.
A holiday feels like eating a big bowl of my favourite ice cream.
A holiday tastes like ice-cold apple juice.

Talitha Harbour
Cameron House School, London

What Is A Holiday?

A holiday smells like sun cream squirting out of the bottle.
A holiday looks like people swimming in the water and playing with the sand.
A holiday sounds like seagulls
And children shouting in the water and playing on the sand.
A holiday feels like sand in my hands and body.
A holiday tastes like ice cream going down my throat.

Giovanni Bertoli (6)
Cameron House School, London

What senses did you enjoy reading about on these pages? Colour the symbols.

Untitled

A conker sounds like *thud!*
A conker tastes yummy
A conker feels hard
A conker smells like outside
A conker is small.

Merlin Taittinger (4)
Cameron House School, London

Untitled

Smells chocolatey
Feels smooth
Sounds lovely
Tastes salty
Looks rough.

Mollie Bradbury (4)
Cameron House School, London

What senses did you enjoy reading about on these pages? Colour the symbols.

Acorns

Acorns smell nice
Taste scrummy
Feel smooth
Sound crunchy
Look round.

Oscar Jackson-Morton (4)
Cameron House School, London

Untitled

A leaf smells like the grass
A leaf tastes crunchy
A leaf feels soft.

Camilla Heitmeyer (4)
Cameron House School, London

What senses did you enjoy reading about on these pages? Colour the symbols.

Untitled

A conker sounds like *bang*
A conker tastes like a tree
A conker feels smooth
A conker smells like mud
A conker is round.

Joseph Priestley (4)
Cameron House School, London

Untitled

Sounds shaky
Feels soft
Tastes chewy
Smells like autumn
Looks spiky.

Nils Kjellberg (4)
Cameron House School, London

What senses did you enjoy reading about on these pages? Colour the symbols.

Autumn

Autumn feels like strong wind
Autumn looks like leaves crunching
Autumn sounds like birds singing
Autumn tastes like marshmallows
Autumn smells like bad mushrooms.

Peter Kearse-Stewart (5)
Cameron House School, London

Autumn

Autumn feels like soft wind.
Autumn looks like lovely houses.
Autumn sounds like friends playing.
Autumn tastes like apple pie.
Autumn smells like muddy puddles.

Oskar Kjellberg (5)
Cameron House School, London

What senses did you enjoy reading about on these pages? Colour the symbols.

Autumn

Autumn feels like crunchy leaves
Autumn looks like windy trees and fireworks
Autumn tastes like apples
Autumn smells like bonfires.

Felipe Egea (5)
Cameron House School, London

Autumn

Autumn feels like crunchy leaves.
Autumn looks like colourful leaves.
Autumn sounds like soft wind.
Autumn tastes like salty rain.
Autumn smells like mushrooms toasting on the fire.

Thibault Lebrun (5)
Cameron House School, London

What senses did you enjoy reading about on these pages? Colour the symbols.

Autumn

Autumn feels like leaves crunching
Autumn looks like bare trees
Autumn sounds like fireworks
Autumn tastes like toasted marshmallows
Autumn smells like hard conkers.

India Cloe Fasciano (6)
Cameron House School, London

Autumn

Autumn feels like crunchy leaves.
Autumn looks like leaves.
Autumn sounds like leaves falling.
Autumn tastes like apple crumble.
Autumn smells like fire.

Atalanta Goulandris (5)
Cameron House School, London

What senses did you enjoy reading about on these pages? Colour the symbols.

My Mum

My mum smells like make-up
My mum looks like a beautiful rose
My mum sounds like angels singing
My mum feels like a cuddly bear
My mum tastes like candyfloss.

Clara-Matthée Rebilly
Cameron House School, London

What Are Fireworks?

Fireworks smell like smoke flying through the air
Fireworks look like colours zooming around the sky
Fireworks sound like guns shooting in the air heavily
Fireworks feel like steam touching your skin
Fireworks taste like sparkling water under bubbles in your mouth.

Matteo Lanza
Cameron House School, London

What senses did you enjoy reading about on these pages? Colour the symbols.

Autumn

Autumn feels like soft wind
Autumn looks like brown leaves
Autumn sounds like crunchy leaves
Autumn tastes like apple pie with marshmallows
Autumn smells like fireworks.

Antonia Trolle
Cameron House School, London

Castles

Castles sound like clinking armour.
Castles look like broken houses.
Castles feel smooth.
Castles smell like old brick
Castles taste like rotten pears.

William Parker (6)
Enborne CE Primary School, Newbury

What senses did you enjoy reading about on these pages? Colour the symbols.

Chocolate

Chocolate tastes like fizz.
Chocolate melts when it's warm.
Chocolate looks like it's fresh.
Chocolate feels like it's melting in my hand.
Chocolate smells like sweets.

Evie May Pearce (6)
Enborne CE Primary School, Newbury

Chocolate

Chocolate sounds like *splish, splosh, splat.*
It is smooth and cold everywhere.
It looks like a brown round cake.
Chocolate smells like a smooth rock.
Chocolate tastes like lots of sugar in my mouth.

Jamie Fry (5)
Enborne CE Primary School, Newbury

What senses did you enjoy reading about on these pages? Colour the symbols.

Autumn

The wind is blowing the flower
We eat apples
I see a robin flying
I smell cheese
I can touch the feathers.

Harry Brewster (6)
Horsted School, Chatham

Autumn

I can hear the crunching noises from the leaves on the ground
I can feel the rough shell of the acorns
I can taste the apples from the trees
I can smell the leaves on the ground
I can see lots of spiderwebs.

David Ebun (6)
Horsted School, Chatham

Untitled

I see trees with no leaves
I taste the leafy wind
I feel the cold wind
I smell the smelly leaves
I hear the crunchy leaves.

Lily Philips (6)
Horsted School, Chatham

Autumn

The trees are blowing where the wind is
The trees are blowing where the leaves are slipping from my fingers
I can smell bonfires in the night
You can pick apples on the trees
Spiders make shimmery webs.

Archie Lee Stafford (7)
Horsted School, Chatham

What senses did you enjoy reading about on these pages? Colour the symbols.

Autumn

Squirrels crunch the leaves
Smooth leaves
I can taste nuts
I can smell leaves
I can see robins.

Luke Micheal Stewart (6)
Horsted School, Chatham

Autumn

You hear leaves crunching
A rough shell of the conkers
The apple trees have lots of fruit
The smell of the harvest food
Pick the apples.

Lexie Woodman (7)
Horsted School, Chatham

What senses did you enjoy reading about on these pages? Colour the symbols.

Autumn

I taste the juice from the apples
I hear the wind blowing from the trees
I can touch the smooth conkers falling from the trees
I can see a creepy branch that has no leaves
I can smell the bonfires.

Mason Matthews (6)
Horsted School, Chatham

Autumn

I can hear the leaves falling off the trees
I can feel rain touching on my soft lovely face
I can smell the harvest fruits
I can taste roasted toast with butter and roasted marshmallows
I can see misty mornings and hedgehogs scrambling in one cosy ball.

Olivia Johnson (6)
Horsted School, Chatham

What senses did you enjoy reading about on these pages? Colour the symbols.

Autumn

A booming thunderstorm
Smoke off the campfire
Bonfires to celebrate the plot
I see hedgehogs wandering around
An acorn in my hand is smooth and soft.

Willow-Rose Cheeseman (6)
Horsted School, Chatham

Autumn

The wind is blowing the trees
Why is the wind stopping?
I can hear leaves swinging through the trees
I can taste apples
I can smell fireworks
I can touch rain on my hands.

Fatima Saeed (7)
Horsted School, Chatham

What senses did you enjoy reading about on these pages? Colour the symbols.

Autumn

I can hear horses riding outside
I can touch a book
I can see fireworks
I can smell orcas
I can taste bananas.

Amy Paul (6)
Horsted School, Chatham

Autumn

I hear the wind
I feel the leaves
I can see the clouds
I smell a bonfire
I taste the food, I eat it cold.

Nathan Davidson (6)
Horsted School, Chatham

Autumn

I can hear the wind rustling
The acorns are falling from the trees
I can see the leaves turning different colours
I can smell a bonfire in the forest
I can taste the burgers.

Nancy Banfield (6)
Horsted School, Chatham

An Autumn Walk

I can see a mummy crow putting juicy, delicious worms in her mouth for her three baby crows
I can smell chicken bones from a barbecue
I can taste the chocolate bar from my pocket that I am eating
I can touch the hard tree bark
I can hear conkers falling off the trees and going *crack!*

Hollie Joanna Kinslow (6)
Horsted School, Chatham

What senses did you enjoy reading about on these pages? Colour the symbols.

An Autumn Walk

I can see spiky hedgehogs
I can smell flowers
I can taste fresh air
I can touch crackling leaves
I can hear hooting.

Dylan Eric Denton (6)
Horsted School, Chatham

An Autumn Walk

I can see colourful leaves
I can smell bonfire smoke
I can taste fresh air
I can touch my woolly scarf
I can hear hooting owls.

Amelie Easton
Horsted School, Chatham

What senses did you enjoy reading about on these pages? Colour the symbols.

An Autumn Walk

I can see a fluffy owl
I can smell boiling fire
I can taste bonfires
I can feel leaves
I can hear crunchy twigs.

Alfie Merritt
Horsted School, Chatham

An Autumn Walk

I can see a soft bunny rabbit
I can feel hedgehogs when I pick them up
I can smell fresh air
I can taste sweet juicy apples
I can hear the wind swishing around.

Grace Hussey
Horsted School, Chatham

What senses did you enjoy reading about on these pages? Colour the symbols.

An Autumn Walk

I can smell fresh air
I can hear the tweeting birds
I can touch the spiky hedgehogs
I can see a hedgehog
I can taste an acorn.

Evie Lola Reynolds (6)
Horsted School, Chatham

An Autumn Walk

I can see bunnies jumping in the air
I can eat the fresh air, it is cold
I can smell bonfires
I can touch crunching leaves under my feet
I can hear owls hooting.

Frankie James Paull (6)
Horsted School, Chatham

What senses did you enjoy reading about on these pages? Colour the symbols.

An Autumn Walk

I can see fluffy owls
I can hear loud thunder claps
I can taste the fresh air
I can touch my warm woolly scarf
I can smell bonfires.

Casey Hunter
Horsted School, Chatham

An Autumn Walk

I can see spiky hedgehogs
I can hear owls hooting
I can taste the fresh air
I can touch slippery logs
I can smell wet leaves.

Sienna Sedge (6)
Horsted School, Chatham

An Autumn Walk

I can see bunny rabbits
I can hear the wind blowing
I can taste sweets from my pocket
I can touch frogs
I can smell wet leaves!

Keira Elise Beswick (6)
Horsted School, Chatham

An Autumn Walk

I can see owls hooting
I can hear hooting owls
I can feel the air
I can smell fresh air
I can taste sweet apples.

Zachary Warsap
Horsted School, Chatham

What senses did you enjoy reading about on these pages? Colour the symbols.

An Autumn Walk

I can see a fluffy rabbit
I can taste the bonfire
I can feel crispy leaves
I can smell smoke
I can hear trees.

Lexi Gilham (6)
Horsted School, Chatham

An Autumn Walk

I can see an owl
I can taste chocolate
I can smell smoke
I can hear the wind in the leaves
I can feel prickly hedgehogs.

Harrison Coxhead
Horsted School, Chatham

What senses did you enjoy reading about on these pages? Colour the symbols.

Autumn Walk

I can see rabbits in the wood
I can smell a bonfire
I can feel leaves. Crunchy!
I can hear the wind.

Finlea Sedge
Horsted School, Chatham

An Autumn Walk

I can see bunnies
I can taste a juicy apple
I can touch a prickly hedgehog
I can smell animals
I can hear hooting owls.

Kayleigh Lees
Horsted School, Chatham

What senses did you enjoy reading about on these pages? Colour the symbols.

An Autumn Walk

I can see a fluffy bunny rabbit
I can smell a smoky bonfire
I can taste juicy apples
I can hear rustling leaves
I can touch brown hedgehogs.

Chloe Cremona
Horsted School, Chatham

An Autumn Walk

I can see owls
I can smell a bonfire
I can taste fresh air
I can hear rustling leaves
I can feel crunchy leaves under my feet.

Paige Pocock (6)
Horsted School, Chatham

What senses did you enjoy reading about on these pages? Colour the symbols.

An Autumn Walk

I can see hedgehogs rolling up
I can smell a campfire
I can taste fresh air
I can touch leaves.

Jaeden Tristan De Jesus (6)
Horsted School, Chatham

An Autumn Walk

I can see big owls speaking to people
I can smell fresh flowers
I can taste fresh mint
I can touch feathers
I can hear people walking around.

Aimee-Louise Harding
Horsted School, Chatham

What senses did you enjoy reading about on these pages? Colour the symbols.

An Autumn Walk

I can see red, yellow and orange leaves
I can smell fresh air
I can taste juicy apples
I can smell squirrels!
I can hear hooting owls.

Katelan May Higgins (7)
Horsted School, Chatham

Forests

Forests look like tall mountains
Forests smell like wet, big apples
Forests sound like birds tweeting
Forests feel like tall, wet, damp trees
Forests taste like stinky, smelly poo.

Reuben Yves-Louis Mundell (6)
Jubilee Primary School, Maidstone

What senses did you enjoy reading about on these pages? Colour the symbols.

Forests

Forests look like long leafy logs
Forests smell like damp fox poo
Forests sound like boys shouting at the football stadium
Forests feel like squelchy mud
Forests taste like soggy sandwiches.

Leon Price (6)
Jubilee Primary School, Maidstone

Forests

Forests look like long, lively leaves
Forests smell like stinky, smelly air
Forests taste like soggy sandwiches
Forests sound like leaves rustling
Forests feel like smooth trees.

Ethan Joubert (7)
Jubilee Primary School, Maidstone

What senses did you enjoy reading about on these pages? Colour the symbols.

Forests

Forests look like dark, damp dirt
Forests smell like fresh tree sap
Forests sound like birds singing
Forests feel like dirty ants
Forests taste like cold wind.

Nathan Molloy (6)
Jubilee Primary School, Maidstone

My Halloween Poem

Halloween sounds like wolves howling
Halloween looks like a haunted house
Halloween tastes like burnt wood
Halloween feels creepy
Halloween smells like hot fire.

Alexander Tottey (6)
Kingsway Primary School, Leicester

What senses did you enjoy reading about on these pages? Colour the symbols.

My Halloween Poem

Halloween is scary like a zombie
but it is fun because I get to party
Halloween is spooky and dark
but it is fun because I get to wear a mask
Halloween is full of squeals
but it gives me fun in my heels
Halloween smells like pumpkin
but I don't like it if it is stinking.

Sulaiman Rahman (6)
Kingsway Primary School, Leicester

My Halloween Poem

Halloween feels scary like a vampire
Halloween looks like haunted houses
Halloween smells like a juicy pumpkin
Halloween sounds like children running in the street
Halloween feels exciting.

Connor O'Sheehan (6)
Kingsway Primary School, Leicester

What senses did you enjoy reading about on these pages? Colour the symbols.

My Halloween Sense Poem

Halloween smells like sugary sweets
Halloween looks like a scary, black vampire
Halloween sounds like scary howling wolves
Halloween feels like frightening ghosts
Halloween looks like magic, spooky, dark witches
Halloween tastes like chocolate and sweets.

Roman Edwards (6)
Kingsway Primary School, Leicester

My Halloween Senses Poem

Halloween sounds like witches cackling
Halloween tastes like sickly sweet treats
Halloween feels spooky and scary
Halloween smells like sweets and candy.

Eman Aslam (6)
Kingsway Primary School, Leicester

My Halloween Senses Poem

Halloween sounds like witches cackling
Halloween tastes like sickly sweet treats
Halloween feels as spooky as a vampire
Halloween smells like melted pumpkins
Halloween looks dark like a haunted house.

Millie Watson (6)
Kingsway Primary School, Leicester

Halloween Senses

Halloween tastes like sweet, yummy candy
Halloween smells like stinky, dark pumpkins
Halloween looks scary as a scared little mouse
Halloween feels scary when you walk past a haunted house
When it's Halloween I can hear children screaming like a dark werewolf
Halloween tastes like yummy sweet sweets
Halloween smells like sticky, yummy treats
At Halloween I can see little kids playing in the garden
Halloween feels scary and creepy.

Keira Anne-Marie Reeve (7)
Kingsway Primary School, Leicester

What senses did you enjoy reading about on these pages? Colour the symbols.

My Halloween Poem

Halloween smells like melted orange juicy pumpkins
Halloween tastes like sickly, yummy sweets
Halloween sounds like crackling fireworks in the sky
Halloween feels exciting
Halloween looks dark like the haunted house
Halloween sounds like the fireworks in the sky
Halloween feels freezing at night
Halloween smells like the chocolate in your basket
Halloween looks like it is really haunted
Halloween feels like spring.

Tegan Parkinson (6)
Kingsway Primary School, Leicester

Here Comes Halloween!

Halloween smells like pumpkins
It looks scary
Sweets taste like warm sweets
I can hear spooky music
I touch hot pumpkin.

Jude King (6)
Kingsway Primary School, Leicester

What senses did you enjoy reading about on these pages? Colour the symbols.

My Halloween Senses Poem

Halloween feels scary like a vampire
Halloween tastes like sugary sweets
Halloween smells like Bonfire Night
Halloween sounds like werewolves howling
Halloween looks like ghosts floating in the air.

Leo Austin Wycherley (7)
Kingsway Primary School, Leicester

My Halloween Poem

Halloween smells like melted chocolate
Halloween sounds like children screaming like a witch
Halloween sounds like a wicked witch scream
Halloween looks like burning hot fire
Halloween looks like hot chocolate
Halloween tastes like melted chocolate
Halloween feels like crunchy toffee sweets
Halloween looks like a vampire dressed up
Halloween looks creepy like spiders everywhere
Halloween looks like a juicy pumpkin.

Dylan Lewis Vaughan (6)
Kingsway Primary School, Leicester

What senses did you enjoy reading about on these pages? Colour the symbols.

My Halloween Poem

Halloween likes scaring people
Halloween smells of orange
Halloween sounds like kids screaming
Halloween is just scary.

Tahlia Marten (6)
Kingsway Primary School, Leicester

Rainy Days

Rain sounds like thunder and loud lightning
Rain smells like wet mud in the grass
Rain tastes like hot chocolate from a nice corner shop
Rain feels like little raindrops
Rain looks like damp clothes
Rain sounds like tip-tapping on the window.

Rebekah Knowles (6)
Kingsway Primary School, Leicester

What senses did you enjoy reading about on these pages? Colour the symbols.

Rainy Days

When it rains I hear thunder cracking in the sky
When it rains it smells of damp mud
When it rains I see wet trees
When it rains I feel cold and wet
When it rains I taste stew and dumplings.

Kayleb Addy (6)
Kingsway Primary School, Leicester

In Summer

In summer you can hear humming like *hum* all day long, I feel sad
In summer you can feel sweat drops raining down your face
In summer you can taste barbecue and ice cream pudding but they're disgusting together
In summer you can see the bright blue sky
In summer you can smell hot dog sausages on a barbecue.

Ella Louise Hayes (6)
Kingsway Primary School, Leicester

What senses did you enjoy reading about on these pages? Colour the symbols.

Beach

I hear seagulls chirping in the distance
I hear waves in the deep blue sea
The waves are made by a whale
People take pictures of sea animals
On the beach you can taste hot dogs, ice cream, Pepsi, Coke and milk
When you are at the beach you can smell seaweed, hot dogs and ice cream
At the beach you see seagulls, sandcastles, sand, sky, strawberry ice cream and crowds of people.
At the beach you can touch the sand, sea, crabs, beach and a beach towel.

Chris Barratt (6)
Kingsway Primary School, Leicester

Untitled

Rain, rain sounds like *drip-drop,*
Rain smells like dirty mud and grass,
Rain tastes like roasted marshmallows,
Rain looks like water falling from the clouds,
Rain feels like wet grass and mud.

Flynn Hill (6)
Kingsway Primary School, Leicester

What senses did you enjoy reading about on these pages? Colour the symbols.

Rainy Days

When it's rainy I can see clouds as dark as coal cover the sky
When it's rainy I can smell wet grass on the flowers
When it's rainy I can taste hot chocolate with marshmallows to keep me warm when it's cold
When it's rainy I can hear rain dripping on the flowers
When it's rainy I can touch wet clothes
When it's rainy I have feelings.

Amelia Chapman (6)
Kingsway Primary School, Leicester

Rainy Days

Rain sounds like raindrops tapping on the window
Rain tastes like real rain off the trees
Rain feels like soggy shoes and socks
Rain looks like white snow and shiny white skates
Rain smells like blue Chewits.

Amy Bodanham (6)
Kingsway Primary School, Leicester

What senses did you enjoy reading about on these pages? Colour the symbols.

Summer Days

In summer I smell hot dogs and ice cream
In summer I see people in swimming pools
In summer I taste Chewits and ice cream
In summer I feel hot cars but I also feel hot sand
I can hear birds.

Ava Kelly (6)
Kingsway Primary School, Leicester

The Rainy Day

Rain sounds very heavy hitting the window of your car
Rain looks like wet, soggy, brown mud all around the ground
Rain reminds me of the lovely taste of hot chocolate
Rain smells like wet, soggy mud
When it rains I can touch very heavy raindrops.

Edward Jones (6)
Kingsway Primary School, Leicester

What senses did you enjoy reading about on these pages? Colour the symbols.

Rainy Day

Rain sounds like soggy, wet raindrops and soggy, wet poo
Lightning sounds like thunder
Damp mud sounds mouldy, wet and soggy
You can smell hot dogs and pepperoni pizza
Tasty, yummy, yummy pizza is damp like damp, soggy, muddy poo
Glass is so sharp.

Ethan Bacon (6)
Kingsway Primary School, Leicester

Rainy Days

Tea and coffee and hot chocolate make you warm like soup and stew and dumplings
I can hear dripping on my door and window
I put up my umbrella
I can smell wet grass
I can smell old wood
I can smell damp
I can smell mud
I can see muddy puddles.

Miley Jade Whitmore (6)
Kingsway Primary School, Leicester

Hot Deserts

In hot deserts you can hear sand dropping in the sea
In hot deserts you can smell new food
In hot deserts I can taste sand in my mouth
In hot deserts I can see water and sand
In hot deserts I can touch sand, water and new food.

Charlie Perrins (7)
Kingsway Primary School, Leicester

Wet, Wet, Wet

Raindrops are wet
Rain is wet and nice
Rain is wet
Rain is like rain
Rain is like wet, wet, wet
Rain is like cold peppers
It is air
Rain is like nice rain
Rain is cold
Rain is wet and cold
Rain is gusty
Rain is not nice
Rain is like sweets
I like rain a lot.

Eva Spencer (6)
Kingsway Primary School, Leicester

What senses did you enjoy reading about on these pages? Colour the symbols.

Rainy Day

Rain tastes like cake
Rain sounds like thunder
Rain feels hot
Rain looks like black clouds
Rain smells like fun
Rain tastes like marshmallows
Rain tastes like wind
Rain feels wet
Rain looks like wolves
Rain smells like mud.

Charlie Lewin (6)
Kingsway Primary School, Leicester

Rainy Days

Rain feels like splashing in puddles
Rain looks like muddy puddles
Rain sounds like *tip-tap* on my head
Rain feels like splashing in puddles.

Talia Bollen (6)
Kingsway Primary School, Leicester

What senses did you enjoy reading about on these pages? Colour the symbols.

A Rainy Day

Rain feels like wet mud squelching in my feet
Rain tastes like melted chocolate in my mouth
Rain looks like soggy branches
Rain smells like wet grass next to me
Rain sounds like thunder and lightning.

Eve Mary Cragg (7)
Kingsway Primary School, Leicester

Rainy Days

Rain sounds like drip-drop
Rain smells like dirty mud and wet grass
Rain tastes like hot chocolate and roasted marshmallows
Rain feels like squelching mud and damp clothes and rain falling down
Rain looks like dark clouds and thunder and lightning.

Abbi Ferrar-Adkin (6)
Kingsway Primary School, Leicester

What senses did you enjoy reading about on these pages? Colour the symbols.

Rain

Rain tastes like marshmallows
Rain sounds like wind blowing through the trees
Rain looks like wellies
Rain feels like damp grass.

Evie Croft (7)
Kingsway Primary School, Leicester

I Can . . .

I can see Hot Wheels cars
I can hear the teacher
I can taste chocolate and doughnuts
I can smell chocolate
I can touch Hot Wheels.

Kurt Jennings (5)
Minworth Junior And Infant School, Sutton Coldfield

What senses did you enjoy reading about on these pages? Colour the symbols.

Outside

I can taste ice cream
I can see the sky, it is blue
I can touch my blanket
I can hear a drum
I can smell flowers.

Millie Woolley
Minworth Junior And Infant School, Sutton Coldfield

If I Was A Superhero

If I was a superhero I could see
All of the birds in the tree
If I was a superhero I could hear
All of the sounds, far or near
If I was a superhero I could taste
All of the things that put a smile on my face
If I was a superhero I could smell
All of the nice things I love so well
If I was a superhero I could touch
All of the animals I love so much.

Lewis Price (7)
Minworth Junior And Infant School, Sutton Coldfield

If I Was A Superhero

If I was a superhero I could see cars driving slowly
If I was a superhero I could hear robbers laughing sneakily
If I was a superhero I could taste the air
If I was a superhero I could smell the bins.

Albert Page (6)
Minworth Junior And Infant School, Sutton Coldfield

If I Was A Superhero

If I was a superhero I would have special powers and fly to the moon and back
And I would have magic stuff in me and you wouldn't know
If I was a superhero I would do silly things
If I was a superhero in the dark would be scary
If I was a superhero I could hear the cars beeping from up above me
If I was a superhero I could hear the perfect people playing up above me
If I was a superhero I would definitely fly with my big muscles.

Lola Evans (7)
Minworth Junior And Infant School, Sutton Coldfield

What senses did you enjoy reading about on these pages? Colour the symbols.

If I Was A Superhero

If I was a superhero I would fly very high in the sky
If I was a superhero I would wear a red top and a blue mask
If I was a superhero I would see all the oceans and I would be kind to others
and if they were in trouble I would save them from the danger
I would be the best at everything
I'd win all the races every day
If I was a superhero I could see all the animals in danger.

Lois May Anderson (7)
Minworth Junior And Infant School, Sutton Coldfield

If I Was A Superhero

If I was a superhero I could see lasers
If I was a superhero I could smell smoke
If I was a superhero I could hear banging on a door
If I was a superhero I could taste a spider.

Lilymay Lacy (5)
Minworth Junior And Infant School, Sutton Coldfield

What senses did you enjoy reading about on these pages? Colour the symbols.

If I Was A Superhero

If I was a superhero I could see the lasers buzzing in my eyes
If I was a superhero I could hear the cars racing on the road
If I was a superhero I could taste the air in my heart
If I was a superhero I could feel the sticky cobwebs.

Jessica Hewitt (6)
Minworth Junior And Infant School, Sutton Coldfield

If I Was A Superhero

If I was a superhero I could see the perfect people from above
If I was a superhero I could hear the cars beeping in the background
If I was a superhero I could feel the breeze blowing
If I was a superhero I could smell the freshly cut grass
If I was a superhero I could taste lizard's blood.

Darcey Casey (6)
Minworth Junior And Infant School, Sutton Coldfield

What senses did you enjoy reading about on these pages? Colour the symbols.

If I Was A Superhero

If I was a superhero I would have a red dress and green hair
If I was a superhero I would be smart
If I was a superhero I would be cheerful
If I was a superhero I would hear the bees
If I was a superhero I would jump really high
If I was a superhero I would mind-control the robbers.

Sophie Shandley (6)
Minworth Junior And Infant School, Sutton Coldfield

If I Was A Superhero

If I was a superhero I could see buildings
If I was a superhero I could hear the robber
If I was a superhero I could taste the cake when I come down
If I was a superhero I could smell the sweets in the shop
If I was a superhero I could touch the windows.

Riley Ian Parry (6)
Minworth Junior And Infant School, Sutton Coldfield

What senses did you enjoy reading about on these pages? Colour the symbols.

If I Was A Superhero

If I was a superhero I could see a beautiful butterfly
If I was a superhero I could hear the robbers laughing loudly
If I was a superhero I could feel a power surge running through my body
If I was a superhero I could smell slithering smoke
If I was a superhero I could taste a doughnut.

Zenun Mezini (7)
Minworth Junior And Infant School, Sutton Coldfield

If I Was A Superhero

If I was a superhero I could see a robber stealing the Queen's throne
If I was a superhero I could hear cars beeping loudly
If I was a superhero I could feel webs shooting out of my hand.

Keira Hobster
Minworth Junior And Infant School, Sutton Coldfield

What senses did you enjoy reading about on these pages? Colour the symbols.

If I Was A Superhero

If I was a superhero I could see the birds
If I was a superhero I could hear the cars
If I was a superhero I could taste the air
If I was a superhero I could smell the food
If I was a superhero I could touch the towers.

Sophie Ann Mills (6)
Minworth Junior And Infant School, Sutton Coldfield

If I Was A Superhero

If I was a superhero I could feel the wall and wind on me
If I was a superhero I could see the beautiful butterfly
If I was a superhero I could hear the cars beeping below me
If I was a superhero I could smell the delicious cakes
If I was a superhero I could taste the windy air.

Jaydee-May Adams (7)
Minworth Junior And Infant School, Sutton Coldfield

What senses did you enjoy reading about on these pages? Colour the symbols.

If I Was A Superhero

If I was a superhero I could see the seagulls
If I was a superhero I could hear the birds tweeting
If I was a superhero I could taste chocolate cake
If I was a superhero I could smell the bins
If I was a superhero I could touch the books.

Keeley Fletcher (6)
Minworth Junior And Infant School, Sutton Coldfield

If I Was A Superhero

If I was a superhero I could see webs
If I was a superhero I could hear the alarms waking people
If I was a superhero I could taste chocolate cake
If I was a superhero I could smell the smoke
If I was a superhero I could touch the moon.

Maddison Maria Carla Doran (6)
Minworth Junior And Infant School, Sutton Coldfield

What senses did you enjoy reading about on these pages? Colour the symbols.

If I Was A Superhero

If I was a superhero I could see flying webs
If I was a superhero I could hear sirens
If I was a superhero I could taste cake
If I was a superhero I could smell chips
If I was a superhero I could touch windows when flying.

Ben Rowbury (6)
Minworth Junior And Infant School, Sutton Coldfield

Five Wonderful Senses

I can see a dog, he is brown.
I can smell the flowers, they are beautiful.
I can touch the horse, she feels soft.
I can hear children tiptoeing, they are cheeky!
I can taste peperoni, it is yummy.

Laila-Marie Harding (6)
Minworth Junior And Infant School, Sutton Coldfield

Untitled

I can hear the trees waving in the wind
I can see the sky, it is blue
I can smell flowers
I can touch the green grass
I can taste yummy chocolate.

Jana Mansour
Minworth Junior And Infant School, Sutton Coldfield

Untitled

I can see a butterfly, it is orange
I can smell the daisies
I can taste the Haribo sweets
I can hear the wind
I can touch a baby, it feels soft.

Savanah Vaughn (6)
Minworth Junior And Infant School, Sutton Coldfield

What senses did you enjoy reading about on these pages? Colour the symbols.

My World

I can see the sea, the sun it is yellow
I can touch and smell the flowers
I can touch a horse
I can taste the chocolate cake
I can hear the birds tweeting.

Shania Loraine Psciuk (6)
Minworth Junior And Infant School, Sutton Coldfield

Declan

I can see a train
I can hear a train
I can taste ice cream
I can smell flowers
I can touch sand.

Declan Rutter-Kilbey
Minworth Junior And Infant School, Sutton Coldfield

What senses did you enjoy reading about on these pages? Colour the symbols.

Untitled

I can see the sun, it is yellow and bright
I can smell flowers, they smell nice
I can taste cookies and drinks
I can hear the wind whooshing through the grass
I can touch everything.

Abigail Warriner
Minworth Junior And Infant School, Sutton Coldfield

Toby's Senses

I can hear the wind crackling in the trees
I can see my classroom, it is full of my friends
I can taste my food and drink
I can feel water washing through my hands.

Toby Richardson (6)
Minworth Junior And Infant School, Sutton Coldfield

What senses did you enjoy reading about on these pages? Colour the symbols.

My Senses

The light is bright I can see it
I can taste dinner, it is yummy
I can smell nice food
I can touch my house, the house is hard.

Chase Cartwright
Minworth Junior And Infant School, Sutton Coldfield

Untitled

I can see toys
I can hear the wind
I can taste ice cream
I can smell flowers
I can touch grass.

Tye Jae Robert Williams
Minworth Junior And Infant School, Sutton Coldfield

What senses did you enjoy reading about on these pages? Colour the symbols.

Poetry In Motion

I can see a red train
I can hear a lot of noise
I can taste mashed potatoes
I can smell smoke from the fire
I can touch my cheek.

William Bird
Minworth Junior And Infant School, Sutton Coldfield

Untitled

I can see the sun, it is a hot sun
I can smell the oranges, they smell nice
I can taste a cake, it is made of chocolate
I can hear a drum banging
I can touch shells, they feel shiny.

Emily Alkiviadou
Minworth Junior And Infant School, Sutton Coldfield

What senses did you enjoy reading about on these pages? Colour the symbols.

Untitled

I can see the yellow sun
I can smell the roses, they are sweet
I can touch the leaves
I can hear the birds
I can taste something yummy
Chocolate is really yummy.

Caidi Pitcher (5)
Minworth Junior And Infant School, Sutton Coldfield

My Senses

I can see the yellow sun
I can hear the ice cream van
I can taste pizza
I can smell pretty flowers
I can touch a green frog.

Shannon Elizabeth Lowe (5)
Minworth Junior And Infant School, Sutton Coldfield

What senses did you enjoy reading about on these pages? Colour the symbols.

Untitled

I can see a green tree
I can hear the trees rustling
I can taste chocolate ice cream
I can smell a roast dinner
I can touch a T-shirt, it's soft.

Holly Haynes-Bradley (5), Ikenna Joel Kevin (6), Tia Mulley & Aimee
Minworth Junior And Infant School, Sutton Coldfield

Untitled

I can see a green tree
I can hear the trees, rough trees rustling
I can taste chocolate ice cream
I can smell a roast dinner
I can touch a trolley, it's hard.

Chloe Abigail Zeff Collin (5) & Logan Rickus (6)
Minworth Junior And Infant School, Sutton Coldfield

What senses did you enjoy reading about on these pages? Colour the symbols.

Untitled

I can smell my cardigan
I can see my hands
I can feel the pencil in my hand
I can taste hot vegetable soup
I can hear a pencil tapping.

Rachelle April (5)
Old Palace of John Whitgift Preparatory School, South Croydon

My Senses

I can smell oranges
I can see scissors
I can feel mud
I can taste candy
I can hear the wind.

Zarina Amzart (5)
Old Palace of John Whitgift Preparatory School, South Croydon

What senses did you enjoy reading about on these pages? Colour the symbols.

Untitled

I can smell sweet fruit
I can see my friend Ellie
I can feel my dress
I can taste pears
I can hear chairs scraping.

Erin Archer (5)
Old Palace of John Whitgift Preparatory School, South Croydon

Untitled

I can smell fish and chips
I can see the shiny tap
I can feel my dress
I can taste potato
I can hear my teacher talking.

Lola Grey (5)
Old Palace of John Whitgift Preparatory School, South Croydon

What senses did you enjoy reading about on these pages? Colour the symbols.

Untitled

I can smell the sweet, juicy fruit
I can see the letters on the wall
I can feel my soft T-shirt
I can taste macaroni cheese
I can hear people walking.

Ellie Thomas (5)
Old Palace of John Whitgift Preparatory School, South Croydon

The World Around Me

I can smell crispy chips
I can see the little pencil pot
I can feel my warm hat
I can taste sandwiches
I can hear my teachers.

Riya Dave (4)
Old Palace of John Whitgift Preparatory School, South Croydon

What senses did you enjoy reading about on these pages? Colour the symbols.

My Very Own Poem

I can smell macaroni and cheese
I can see my friend, Erin
I can feel soft, bendy Play-Doh
I can taste cheesy pasta
I can hear the bell going back and forth.

Amanah Lone (4)
Old Palace of John Whitgift Preparatory School, South Croydon

Childhood

I can smell food
I can see flowers
I can feel sticky sugar doughnuts
I can taste noodle soup
I can hear the children.

Anne Marie Arava (4)
Old Palace of John Whitgift Preparatory School, South Croydon

Untitled

I can smell soft cheese
I can see my teacher
I can feel the sharp pencil
I can taste jam cake
I can hear talking.

Niamh O'Connor-Batchelor (4)
Old Palace of John Whitgift Preparatory School, South Croydon

Untitled

I can smell chicken biryani
I can see my friend, Amanah
I can feel hot
I can taste pasta
I can hear birds.

Aashita Sharma (4)
Old Palace of John Whitgift Preparatory School, South Croydon

What senses did you enjoy reading about on these pages? Colour the symbols.

Winter

I can see snow falling from the sky
People love making snowmen too
And like to dress them up
I can taste warm hot chocolate in my mouth,
It's really hot but yummy
I can hear people saying, 'Thank you' to Santa Claus
I can touch my warm, snuggly blanket
And cuddle up to it.

Safiya Ukani (6)
Old Palace of John Whitgift Preparatory School, South Croydon

My Biscuits

My biscuits smell like strawberry jam
My biscuits taste like crunchy shortbread
My biscuits feel like smooth icing
My biscuits look like beautiful hearts
My biscuits sound like chomping children.

Isobel Binacchi (6)
Old Palace of John Whitgift Preparatory School, South Croydon

What senses did you enjoy reading about on these pages? Colour the symbols.

Irresistible Chocolate

Chocolate feels like a smooth, squidgy, silky and firm snack
I can see a glossy white bar of chocolate, a big light surprise
I snap my chocolate in half
I break a bit off it and crunch it slowly
Chocolate tastes like a Sunny Delight, a cheery, milky delight
Chocolate smells like an irresistible meal
Sweet, delicious fragrant nuts in a bar of chocolate
Which is going to be eaten all up.

Rhianna Davids-Shaw (6)
Old Palace of John Whitgift Preparatory School, South Croydon

Ice Cream Dream

I love ice cream
Ice cream tastes like a dream
Strawberries smell sweet
But chocolate is a treat
I can hear the ice cream van
And I can see the ice cream man
Children are playing at the seaside
And children are going for a bike ride
I can feel the hot, hot sun
But eating ice cream is much more fun
I run to get the gooey, melting ice cream
Ice cream is definitely a dream.

Carys Dhonota (6)
Old Palace of John Whitgift Preparatory School, South Croydon

What senses did you enjoy reading about on these pages? Colour the symbols.

Dynamic Dave

He smells of bravery
and he can't stand slavery.

He feels hard on the outside
but he is gentle and friendly on the inside.

Zoom! Zoom! Zoom! he sounds
whenever help is needed
Dave speeds off to get there quick.

I see him always beaming
even when he's fighting the bad
he is never sad.

He tastes like fresh veg and fruit
because he eats salad to keep healthy
Dynamic Dave's always brave and eager to save.

Ewaoluwayimika Fayokun (6)
Old Palace of John Whitgift Preparatory School, South Croydon

What senses did you enjoy reading about on these pages? Colour the symbols.

Spring! Oh Spring!

Spring is lovely weather for plants to sow
Spring is when blossom starts to grow
Spring is a season when it never rains
Spring is when happiness never ends

Spring is when the sun is shining in the sky
I wish it never stops shining
Spring is when the weather stays calm
Spring is when baby lambs are born

Spring is sunny, warm and bright to play in
Spring is more exciting than crisps
In spring birds chirp in groups

Spring is a weather of roses; it reminds me of pink silk
Spring smells like Easter eggs, yum-yum in my tum
Spring sounds like children playing on the sea waves

Spring is the best season ever!
I wish it ends never!

Nikhita Sambre (6)
Old Palace of John Whitgift Preparatory School, South Croydon

What senses did you enjoy reading about on these pages? Colour the symbols.

Winter

Winter smells fresh and clean
Winter looks like snowflakes, bright and white
Winter feels like cold, squashy snow
Winter is white
And I can hear a snowball fight
Winter, I can taste warm Ribena.

Jorjah Siena Walters (6)
Old Palace of John Whitgift Preparatory School, South Croydon

Happiness

Happiness makes me laugh
Happiness comes when I see a fluttering butterfly
Happiness makes me feel joyful
Happiness makes me smell wonderful, blooming pink flowers
I feel happiness when I hear birds chirping
Happiness is all around us, I feel happy.

Aabisha Kandasamy (6)
Old Palace of John Whitgift Preparatory School, South Croydon

What senses did you enjoy reading about on these pages? Colour the symbols.

Doughnuts

D oughnuts are round, sticky and sweet, fun to eat
O range-flavoured doughnuts with sprinkles are my favourite to eat
U sually you find them in the shops to buy and eat
G reat for sharing with my friends as a treat
H ear them bubbling away in the frying pan, soon to eat
N ot to be eaten all the time as they ruin your teeth
U ncooked doughnuts smell like old cheese and are not good to eat
T hey taste delicious with whipped cream and a chocolate treat
S haring doughnuts brings a smile to all who eat.

Daya Chana (7)
Old Palace of John Whitgift Preparatory School, South Croydon

Owls

I can hear the owl tweeting and singing
I can touch the owl's soft feathers and warm body
I can see the owl flapping her large wings and I can see her perching on the branches
I wonder what the owl had for lunch and what it tasted like
I can smell the sweet and fresh breeze when she flaps her wings.

Zoha Mirza (6)
Old Palace of John Whitgift Preparatory School, South Croydon

What senses did you enjoy reading about on these pages? Colour the symbols.

Cute, Fluffy Cats

Some cats look cute and fluffy
Some cats are grumpy
Cats smell like a rainy day
Cats feel as soft as silk
Cats go *miaow, miaow, miaow* when they are hungry
I'm sure they taste just as good as chicken!

Amber Grace Nodder (7)
Old Palace of John Whitgift Preparatory School, South Croydon

Africa

Africa smells like mud stuck to the bottom of my wellies
And strong spices from Grandma's delicious cooking
Africa feels sweaty and sticky
Makes me want to peel my clothes off
Africa sounds like drivers shouting and beeping their horns
Cocks crowing, *coo, coo, coo* and owls hooting, *hoo, hoo, hoo*
Africa looks like a rainbow
Colourful coconut, sour sop, mango and orange trees
Africa tastes like juicy oranges dripping down my hands on a boiling hot summer day.

Sapphy Oboh (6)
Old Palace of John Whitgift Preparatory School, South Croydon

What senses did you enjoy reading about on these pages? Colour the symbols.

Lemon Drizzle Cake

The thing I like my mum to bake is yummy lemon drizzle cake
I hear the whisk go round and round. What a lovely sound
The lemon smells so sweet. This is going to be a treat
The house is filled with this delicious air
I cannot wait, this is not fair
The cake is soft and smooth and golden brown, if only I could taste it now
I feel the heat from the baking tray
This could be a little tricky, it looks so good and feels so sticky
Finally it's time to eat, what a very scrumptious treat
The crunchy top, the spongy middle
The cake is sweet, the plate is clean
The cleanest it has ever been
There is nothing left to say right now but mmm, wow!

Your poem has been chosen as the best in this book!

Tahlyah O'Brady (6)
Old Palace of John Whitgift Preparatory School, South Croydon

Ice Cream

Ice cream smells like a cold winter breeze
Ice cream looks like the sky falling down and changing colours
Ice cream sounds like a small girl screaming
Ice cream feels like the cold, wet and soggy
Ice cream tastes like chocolate, coffee, toffee, Oreos, bubblegum and strawberry.

Aarna Wangoo (6)
Old Palace of John Whitgift Preparatory School, South Croydon

What senses did you enjoy reading about on these pages? Colour the symbols.

Chocolate Is . . .

Chocolate looks like a brown tree trunk
Chocolate feels like a slippery brown rock
Chocolate smells like a melted ice cream
Chocolate sounds like a big brown rock breaking
Chocolate tastes like melted caramel and chocolate cake.

Heidi Martin (6)
Palace Wood Primary School, Maidstone

Chocolate

Chocolate looks like a shape; shiny and different shades of brown and white
Chocolate smells as sweet as ripe strawberries
Chocolate feels as sharp as a mountain top on your tongue when you bite into it
Chocolate tastes like a caramel twirl
Chocolate feels like a melting candle in the sunlight
Chocolate sounds as crunchy as a Crunchie bar.

Amelia Burchill (7)
Palace Wood Primary School, Maidstone

What senses did you enjoy reading about on these pages? Colour the symbols.

Chocolate

Chocolate looks as shiny as a crystal
Chocolate tastes as sweet as a yummy candy cane
Chocolate feels cold and squishy
Chocolate sounds like the crackling fire
Chocolate smells as sweet as strawberries
Chocolate looks as tasty as sugar
Chocolate tastes as lovely as roses.

Cooper Bedford (7)
Palace Wood Primary School, Maidstone

Chocolate

Chocolate smells chocolatey
Chocolate looks like bronze
Chocolate snaps, dribbles, slides and is pointy
Chocolate feels as hot as hot water
Chocolate tastes like chocolate
Chocolate smells like sweets
Chocolate looks like a brick
Chocolate feels like roses.

Zara Ian Foulsham (6)
Palace Wood Primary School, Maidstone

What senses did you enjoy reading about on these pages? Colour the symbols.

I Sense Spring

In spring I can smell flowers
I can see leaves
I can hear crunching
I can feel the breeze.

Elisiya Francois Hector (6)
Palace Wood Primary School, Maidstone

Winter

You can see the leaves all around you
You can smell the snow
You can hear the snow
You feel colder
You can taste snow.

Levie Smith (6)
Palace Wood Primary School, Maidstone

What senses did you enjoy reading about on these pages? Colour the symbols.

Chocolate Is . . .

Chocolate looks as if it's the brownest and yummiest thing in the world
Chocolate feels as smooth as smooth could be
Chocolate smells like a sweet and sugary breeze
Chocolate sounds like a scrumptious and crunchy noise
Chocolate tastes like gooey and sticky bumps in your mouth.

Tom McIvor (7)
Palace Wood Primary School, Maidstone

Chocolate Is . . .

Chocolate looks like brown pants
Chocolate feels smooth and soft
Chocolate smells like chocolate custard
Chocolate sounds like crunching in your mouth
Chocolate tastes like sticky chocolate.

Finley King (6)
Palace Wood Primary School, Maidstone

What senses did you enjoy reading about on these pages? Colour the symbols.

Untitled

In the spring I can smell smoky air
I can see flowers
I can feel soft flowers
I can taste hot chocolate
I can hear birds singing songs.

Noah Cruickshank (5)
Palace Wood Primary School, Maidstone

Autumn

In the autumn:
I can see trees
I can hear the wind blow the leaves
I can feel the leaves
I can smell the dead leaves
I can taste a drink.

Emilia Seren Cruz (5)
Palace Wood Primary School, Maidstone

What senses did you enjoy reading about on these pages? Colour the symbols.

My First Day

I saw a yellow and red train on the playground
I could smell shampoo
I could hear children chattering loudly
I like tasting rain
I think I'm going to love it at St Ben's, my new school!

Teegan Balbini (6)
St Benedict's Catholic Primary School, Warrington

The Isle Of Struay

I hear the ocean
I taste the wind
I smell the ocean breeze
I see Grannie Mainland coming on the boat
I feel the boat moving.

Isabelle Clements (7)
St Benedict's Catholic Primary School, Warrington

What senses did you enjoy reading about on these pages? Colour the symbols.

The Isle Of Struay

On Struay it is noisy
On Struay it tastes like salty seaweed
On Struay it smells of pasta
On Struay I can touch a table
On Sturay I can see water, boats and clover.

Jenson Coleman-King (6)
St Benedict's Catholic Primary School, Warrington

The Isle Of Struay

Struay smells like seaweed
It tastes like sausage
I hear singing from a village
I can touch the ground and a tree
I can see a village.

Maja Machowicz (6) & Paulina
St Benedict's Catholic Primary School, Warrington

What senses did you enjoy reading about on these pages? Colour the symbols.

The Isle Of Struay

I can hear breezy, strong wind whizzing across my ears, the wind makes my strong, lovely hair blow!
I can taste salty, soggy seaweed with creamy chocolate cake, even the great cheesy crisps!
You can smell the sweet smell of mango!
You can feel hard, deep, wooden wood and feel the softest bed in the world!
You can see a gloomy brick house and the old farm!

Tristan Achu (7)
St Benedict's Catholic Primary School, Warrington

The Isle Of Struay

I can hear the trees rustling
I can touch the jetty
I can see a house
I can smell seaweed
I can taste salt and wind.

Imogen Louise Kelsall (6)
St Benedict's Catholic Primary School, Warrington

What senses did you enjoy reading about on these pages? Colour the symbols.

The Isle Of Struay

Struay smells like salty seaweed and oranges and food
Struay sounds like screaming and the water making waves
In Struay, you can see the seagulls fly in the air, the fish, the sun, the Post Office and the new house.

Oscar Edward Miller (6)
St Benedict's Catholic Primary School, Warrington

Struay

Struay sounds like birds singing
Struay smells like mouldy fish
Struay looks like a beautiful island
Struay feels like muddy puddles
Struay tastes like vinegar and salty seaweed.

Ben Pham (7)
St Benedict's Catholic Primary School, Warrington

Struay

Struay smells like salty seaweed
Seagulls up in the air
Fish swimming in the sea
Birds fly up in the air.

Alexandra MacMillan (6)
St Benedict's Catholic Primary School, Warrington

The Isle Of Struay

When I am in Struay I can hear the breeze and trees
And on Struay I can touch the wall
And on Struay I can taste the seaweed, the salty seaweed
And I see islands and people.

Josh Ackerley (7)
St Benedict's Catholic Primary School, Warrington

What senses did you enjoy reading about on these pages? Colour the symbols.

Isle Of Struay

I can see the lighthouse
I can see the rocks
I can smell the fish and the water
I can hear fish, waves and dolphins
I can feel the salty, salty water on my toes as I walk on the sand.

Jack Van-Dusen (6)
St Benedict's Catholic Primary School, Warrington

Struay

When I was on Struay I felt the wind
Struay smells of seaweed
On Struay I always see people
On Struay I always hear the jetty
It's really good in Struay
I went on the jetty
It is really good on the jetty
I touched the side of the jetty
It's really funny when seagulls fly above your head.

Milly Elmore (6)
St Benedict's Catholic Primary School, Warrington

What senses did you enjoy reading about on these pages? Colour the symbols.

The Island Of Struay

It smells beautiful
I can taste the seaweed
On Struay the sea smells like seaweed
I can hear the water
I can feel the lighthouse
I can see the Post Office and Katie-Morag.

Grace Cragg (7)
St Benedict's Catholic Primary School, Warrington

The Isle Of Struay

The cars are loud, the jetty is very loud too
It is very cold but still sunny
It smells beautifully perfect
It tastes like seaweed.

William Pritchard
St Benedict's Catholic Primary School, Warrington

What senses did you enjoy reading about on these pages? Colour the symbols.

The Isle Of Struay

When I am on Struay I hear the breeze and trees wobbling
And on Struay I can smell the seaweed
But what I can see is the sea
What I can taste is the seaweed.

Oliver Junior Bedford (7)
St Benedict's Catholic Primary School, Warrington

The Isle Of Struay

Struay smells like salty seaweed and the sea
Struay tastes of food and seaweed
Struay sounds like seagulls and houses and the jetty too
Struay looks like all the houses and streetlights and the island on the jetty.

Cole Thomas Ashcroft-Burgess (6)
St Benedict's Catholic Primary School, Warrington

What senses did you enjoy reading about on these pages? Colour the symbols.

The Isle Of Struay

On the Isle of Struay you can hear the flowing waves coming from the ocean
On the Isle of Struay you can touch the big, white ferry about to start
On the Isle of Struay you can taste the big, blue sky
On the Isle of Struay you can smell the sweet sea salt
On the Isle of Struay you can see the friendly Post Office.

Charlotte Hilton (7)
St Benedict's Catholic Primary School, Warrington

The Isle Of Struay

I can see people planting
I can feel a jumper that's soft
I can hear a breeze
I can taste seaweed
I can smell a breeze.

Zachary Maddock
St Benedict's Catholic Primary School, Warrington

What senses did you enjoy reading about on these pages? Colour the symbols.

The Isle Of Struay

Struay feels like a salty land and it's very windy!
Struay tastes like the breeze coming through your mouth when your lips are still together
On Struay you can hear the seagulls flying over your head, it's very funny
On Struay you can see all the cars whizzing by
On Struay you can smell salty seaweed.

Austin White (6)
St Benedict's Catholic Primary School, Warrington

The Isle Of Struay

Struay smells like seaweed and fish
Next I hear a car on Struay
Then I touch the jetty
I see it with people
I can taste chocolate.

Lore Omotosho (6)
St Benedict's Catholic Primary School, Warrington

What senses did you enjoy reading about on these pages? Colour the symbols.

The Isle Of Struay

Struay tastes like oranges
Struay smells like hot chocolate
On Struay you can hear the jetty
On Struay you can touch the jetty
On Struay you can see the ocean.

Noah Whitlow (6)
St Benedict's Catholic Primary School, Warrington

Autumn Poem

Conker, conker
Low and low
Falling from
The tree.

Ollie Kai Callaghan (5)
St Ebbe's CE (Aided) Primary School, Oxford

Autumn Poem

Conkers falling with the wind
Higher and higher
Smell of fire.

Matteo Giulio Ferrari-Pastorino (5)
St Ebbe's CE (Aided) Primary School, Oxford

Autumn Poem

Falling
Twirling
Curling leaves
Blowing
Whooshing
From the trees.

Saif Rana
St Ebbe's CE (Aided) Primary School, Oxford

What senses did you enjoy reading about on these pages? Colour the symbols.

Autumn Poem

Whooshing, whooshing
Wind spin
Autumn leaves
Glowing yellow
From the tree.

Marc Zhi-Bin Oldfield (5)
St Ebbe's CE (Aided) Primary School, Oxford

Autumn Poem

Croak, ribbit
Birds tweet
Fly, fly
Rainbow in the sky.

David Ezenva
St Ebbe's CE (Aided) Primary School, Oxford

Autumn Poem

Acorn
Higher and higher
Can you smell fire?
Leaves tall
Conkers, conkers
Fall gold.

Anoushka Tong
St Ebbe's CE (Aided) Primary School, Oxford

Autumn Poem

Snappy
Crack
Red leaves
Leaves
Apples
From the trees.

Rafael Velazquez
St Ebbe's CE (Aided) Primary School, Oxford

What senses did you enjoy reading about on these pages? Colour the symbols.

Autumn Poem

Red
Crunchy
Green leaves
Crack
Twirl
From the trees.

Hamza Miah
St Ebbe's CE (Aided) Primary School, Oxford

Autumn Poem

Crying blackbirds
Dancing in the sky
Blue sky
Orange trees
White clouds.

Alisha Sadiq
St Ebbe's CE (Aided) Primary School, Oxford

What senses did you enjoy reading about on these pages? Colour the symbols.

Autumn Poem

Swirling leaves
Swirling leaves are falling
From the trees.

Elizaveta Mullaney (5)
St Ebbe's CE (Aided) Primary School, Oxford

Autumn Poem

Dom the squirrel
Saw a nut
That was shiny
Way up in the sky.

Dominic Szlama
St Ebbe's CE (Aided) Primary School, Oxford

Autumn Poem

Falling leaves
Yellow and red and golden and orange fall
Lots of leaves fall all day
People are singing
Wind is blowing
Blackberries are growing
Hedgehogs are hibernating.

Mahtab Mansoorian
St Ebbe's CE (Aided) Primary School, Oxford

Autumn Poem

Leaves fall off the trees
Hedgehogs eat leaves
A rabbit comes out and eats carrots from the garden.

Enrico Siruntie Lewis (6)
St Ebbe's CE (Aided) Primary School, Oxford

What senses did you enjoy reading about on these pages? Colour the symbols.

Autumn Poem

Falling leaves swirling
Autumn leaves twirling
I love autumn
Squirrels are collecting acorns
I love autumn.

Daisy Puttick
St Ebbe's CE (Aided) Primary School, Oxford

Autumn Poem

Yellow and red leaves
That you will soon find
Hedgehogs come out.

Hannah Atkinson
St Ebbe's CE (Aided) Primary School, Oxford

Autumn Poem

Hedgehogs come
Hedgehogs come outside
I love autumn
Hedgehogs come out in autumn
Squirrels come out in autumn.

Rose Evelyn Grace Martin (5)
St Ebbe's CE (Aided) Primary School, Oxford

Autumn Poem

Conkers crack
And people cheer and leaves
Fall from the tree.

Bianca Zanetti
St Ebbe's CE (Aided) Primary School, Oxford

What senses did you enjoy reading about on these pages? Colour the symbols.

Autumn Poem

An autumn day is the orange leaves that are falling
And conkers coming to the ground
If my leaves are falling so are all the leaves on an autumn day.

Trinity Mukamasobola (5)
St Ebbe's CE (Aided) Primary School, Oxford

Pop Pop Sizzle

My name is Ellie and I love jelly
It's not smelly and it fills my belly
Sometimes I eat jelly while I watch telly
My name is Ellie Jelly Belly.

Ellie Lilly-May Levermore (5)
St Osyth CE Primary School, Clacton-On-Sea

What senses did you enjoy reading about on these pages? Colour the symbols.

Autumn's Coming

Clouds as fluffy as candyfloss
Wind blowing in the trees
Smoky bonfires ready for marshmallows
Leaves as crunchy as sweet wrappers
Mum's shepherd's pie tastes scrumptious.

Lyla Symonds
St Osyth CE Primary School, Clacton-On-Sea

Untitled

Christmas looks like a snow day
Christmas sounds like crunching leaves
Christmas tastes like snow
Christmas smells like a cold day
Christmas feels like playing.

Lacey Thomas (6)
St Osyth CE Primary School, Clacton-On-Sea

What senses did you enjoy reading about on these pages? Colour the symbols.

Christmas

Christmas looks like white snowflakes
Christmas looks like a big, fat turkey
Christmas feels like Mummy's hands.

Jersey Megan Woodcraft (6)
St Osyth CE Primary School, Clacton-On-Sea

Christmas

It looks like white clouds
It sounds like it's crunchy
It tastes soggy
It smells like air.

Ronnie Lucas Euripidou (6)
St Osyth CE Primary School, Clacton-On-Sea

What senses did you enjoy reading about on these pages? Colour the symbols.

Christmas

Christmas looks like birds singing
Christmas sounds like trees
Christmas tastes like chicken
Christmas smells like an angel
Christmas feels like crunchy leaves.

Georgia Sofia Green (6)
St Osyth CE Primary School, Clacton-On-Sea

Christmas

Christmas looks special
Christmas sounds like ice
Christmas smells like cream
Christmas feels like us.

Jayden Gray (6)
St Osyth CE Primary School, Clacton-On-Sea

What senses did you enjoy reading about on these pages? Colour the symbols.

Christmas Poem

Christmas looks like an old lady
Christmas sounds like falling snow
Christmas tastes like Cornetto ice cream
Christmas smells like ice cream.

Ben Headford (6)
St Osyth CE Primary School, Clacton-On-Sea

Christmas

Christmas looks like a rusty boat
Christmas sounds like wind whistling
Christmas tastes like sweet fresh sweets
Christmas smells like stinky mud
Christmas feels like soft pillows.

Brooke Smith (6)
St Osyth CE Primary School, Clacton-On-Sea

What senses did you enjoy reading about on these pages? Colour the symbols.

Christmas

Christmas looks like fires
Christmas sounds like crunching leaves
Christmas tastes like ice and snow
Christmas smells like spaghetti
Christmas feels like 23 ants.

Archie Rogers (6)
St Osyth CE Primary School, Clacton-On-Sea

My Dog . . .

My dog likes being stroked
My dog tastes disgusting
My dog likes to bark
My dog has black and white fur
I love my dog.

Merson-Lucas Griggs (6)
St Osyth CE Primary School, Clacton-On-Sea

What senses did you enjoy reading about on these pages? Colour the symbols.

Christmas

Christmas looks like ice
Christmas tastes like snow
Christmas feels like you're home in bed
Christmas sounds like fog.

Sophie-Rose Lund-Conlon (5)
St Osyth CE Primary School, Clacton-On-Sea

Christmas Poem

Christmas looks like lots of fun
Christmas feels like Christmas presents
Christmas tastes like Christmas pudding
Christmas smells like mince pies
Christmas sounds like jingle bells.

Irene Hook (5)
St Osyth CE Primary School, Clacton-On-Sea

What senses did you enjoy reading about on these pages? Colour the symbols.

All About Me

I like to taste chocolate bars
I like to touch dogs
I can hear lions roaring
I can see a panda climbing a tree
I can see a bin
I see children on the carpet.

Timilehin Ayorinde (5)
St Paul's and All Hallows CE Junior School, London

Myself

I like looking at dogs
I like smelling candyfloss
I like tasting cheeseburgers
I like listening to peaceful music
I like playing
I like touching creatures.

Joshua Thomas-Wanliss (5)
St Paul's and All Hallows CE Junior School, London

What senses did you enjoy reading about on these pages? Colour the symbols.

I Can . . .

I can see a cat stuck in the tree
I can hear a dog barking
I can touch a cat
I can taste grapes
I can smell lunch.

Justice Obeng-Hammond (5)
St Paul's and All Hallows CE Junior School, London

I Like . . .

I can feel a lion
I can smell a dog
I can see a hot sun
I can taste lollipops
I can hear a TV.

Jada Rose Ebony Oti-Sampson (5)
St Paul's and All Hallows CE Junior School, London

What senses did you enjoy reading about on these pages? Colour the symbols.

Myself

I can see birds
I can smell flowers
I can taste chips
I can hear a bird
I can feel grass.

Ana Mustata (5)
St Paul's and All Hallows CE Junior School, London

Myself

I can feel tables
I can see boards
I can smell nice food
I can taste beans
I can hear aeroplanes.

Cameron Mckenzie (5)
St Paul's and All Hallows CE Junior School, London

What senses did you enjoy reading about on these pages? Colour the symbols.

My Season

Autumn looks like fireworks and pumpkins in the middle of the night
Autumn smells like chocolate soup
Autumn tastes like toffee apples and porridge
Autumn sounds like terrible storms and rain
Autumn feels like crunchy, juicy leaves.

Betelhiem Kibrom (6)
St Paul's and All Hallows CE Junior School, London

Myself

I like to hear dogs
I like to feel my toes
I like to smell chicken
I like to taste curry goat
I like to see my brother.

Ayanna Johnson (6)
St Paul's and All Hallows CE Junior School, London

What senses did you enjoy reading about on these pages? Colour the symbols.

Myself

I like to see monkeys,
I like to taste tasty food,
I like to feel terrifying dinosaurs,
I like to smell nice banana,
I like to hear the breeze!

Kyri Nicolaou (5)
St Paul's and All Hallows CE Junior School, London

My Season

Autumn smells like pumpkins in the air and clouds
Autumn tastes like toffee apples, I can eat them all day
Autumn feels like crunchy, colourful leaves on the ground
Autumn sounds like rain dripping out of my ears
Autumn looks like beautiful, blossoming flowers growing
Lots of what is blossoming is also falling.

Mikel Joseph Alexander (7)
St Paul's and All Hallows CE Junior School, London

What senses did you enjoy reading about on these pages? Colour the symbols.

My Season

I can touch light that is really, really bright
I can see blossoms that are coming down to sleep
I can smell garbage
Sugar tastes like bombs and sweets, I will enjoy one sweet
I can feel some whoopee cushions, I hope you can feel some too
I can hear solid merchants cheer
I can smell fireworks, can you?
I can taste pumpkin soup, can you?

Stephen Adjei (6)
St Paul's and All Hallows CE Junior School, London

My Season

In autumn you can hear birds chirping to everyone saying, 'Wake up!'
Autumn feels like brown leaves tumbling down trees
Autumn looks like squirrels getting nuts
Autumn smells like a cool breeze
Autumn tastes like the wind of autumn.

Nicholas Brimah (7)
St Paul's and All Hallows CE Junior School, London

What senses did you enjoy reading about on these pages? Colour the symbols.

My Season

Autumn sounds like crunchy leaves
Autumn tastes like rice and cheese
Autumn smells like fish and lemon
and that makes me laugh for twenty seconds
Autumn looks like clouds swooping beside me
Autumn feels like wood logs
I'm about to scream!

Malaika Ameyaw (6)
St Paul's and All Hallows CE Junior School, London

My Season

Autumn smells like the black and white bees flashing in the rain
Autumn looks like the white, blue sky moving as slow as the three little brown round leaves
Autumn feels like dark, thundery rain dripping on my head
Autumn sounds like all the flying birds passing by.

Jatian Dumbuya (6)
St Paul's and All Hallows CE Junior School, London

What senses did you enjoy reading about on these pages? Colour the symbols.

My Season

Autumn smells like fireworks and wind
Autumn looks like bashing fireworks exploding in the sky
Autumn sounds like leaves under my feet
Autumn feels windy, foggy and squidgy under my feet
Autumn leaves feel like sandpaper
Autumn tastes like pumpkin soup and chocolate chips.

Troy O'Neil (7)
St Paul's and All Hallows CE Junior School, London

My Season

I can feel rain falling down to the ground
Autumn looks like the wind is swishing
Autumn tastes like juicy pumpkins
Autumn smells like chestnuts
I can hear the crunchy leaves
The squirrels are crunching and munching the leaves
When the trees fall down it is swishing around the whole place.

Joshua Moh-Okwara (7)
St Paul's and All Hallows CE Junior School, London

What senses did you enjoy reading about on these pages? Colour the symbols.

My Season

Autumn smells like sweet, juicy apples
I can eat them all day
In the middle of May
Autumn tastes like red, wobbly jelly
And the name is Kelly
I can touch furry rabbits
Jumping around on the ground
In autumn I can see brown squirrels
Jumping all around.

Angela Sarfo (6)
St Paul's and All Hallows CE Junior School, London

My Season

In my ears, autumn is in my ears
The wind is blowing heavily
Autumn tastes like chocolate salt with tumbling rain
Autumn smells like roasting pumpkin and chestnuts
Autumn feels like crushing, munching leaves
Autumn looks like loud clapping fireworks.

Zenayah Walker (6)
St Paul's and All Hallows CE Junior School, London

What senses did you enjoy reading about on these pages? Colour the symbols.

My Season

Autumn smells like pumpkin soup and coffee in my nose
I can hear bonfires bombing in the air
Everything reminds me of autumn, it is fun to celebrate
I can see squirrels on the trees picking up acorns
I can taste the chocolate roasting on the fire.

Favour Kader Sheriff (6)
St Paul's and All Hallows CE Junior School, London

My Season

I can hear autumn scream
I can taste juicy cake
I can touch autumn's cold leaves
I can smell lovely air
I can see leaves dropping on my head
Maybe I can see it again.

Meba Fasika (6)
St Paul's and All Hallows CE Junior School, London

What senses did you enjoy reading about on these pages? Colour the symbols.

Young Writers Information

We hope you have enjoyed reading this book – and that you will continue to in the coming years.

If you're a young writer who enjoys reading and creative writing, or the parent of an enthusiastic poet or story writer, do visit our website **www.youngwriters.co.uk**. Here you will find free competitions, workshops and games, as well as recommended reads, a poetry glossary and our blog.

If you would like to order further copies of this book, or any of our other titles give us a call or visit **www.youngwriters.co.uk**.

Young Writers
Remus House
Coltsfoot Drive
Peterborough
PE2 9BF

(01733) 890066
info@youngwriters.co.uk